This booklet is for you: the hospital patient; the one who is ill; your family; your friends and those who attend to your needs. Its message comes from traditional and modern sources, combining the past and present to bring comfort and strength.

שערי רפואה

Gates
of
Healing

They who wait for God
  shall renew their strength,
  they shall mount up with wings like eagles,
they shall run and not be weary,
  they shall walk and not faint.
  — *Isaiah*

Tenth printing 2005

ISBN 0-88123-005-7

CCAR Press
355 Lexington Avenue
New York, New York 10017

The family and friends of Sidney (Shalom) Winnig are proud to sponsor the publication of *Gates of Healing*. It is dedicated in memory of a man who walked through life proudly with his family and humbly with his God. He lived with honor, dignity and a strong belief in Judaism. During his lifetime he devoted himself to serving his God and his people through his many charitable acts. He felt there should be a work available which would reflect the spirit and traditions of Reform Judaism to which people could turn for comfort. *Gates of Healing* is the work he envisioned. It is our hope that the readers will find the consolation and inspiration they seek.

The Family and Friends of Sidney Winnig,
Rosh Hashana, 5749.

The Central Conference of American Rabbis also acknowledges with deep gratitude the contributions of the many rabbis whose devotion, wisdom and insight are reflected in these pages. We particularly thank:

Rabbis Hirshel L. Jaffe and H. Leonard Poller, for compiling the final edition of this book;

Rabbis William Sajowitz and Jordan Pearlson, whose early research and writings brought this project into being, and provided the basis for the current work;

Rabbi Herbert Bronstein, former Chair of the Liturgy Committee, for his encouragement.

Rabbi Joseph Levine, whose gentle persuasion as chair of the Health Committee eased the project along at critical moments.

Several meditations have also been used from *Looking Up While Lying Down*, by John E. Biegert (Pilgrim Press, 1978).

THE PATHWAY TO GOD

Prayer is a pathway to God
which leads us to feel God's love,
not only in the heavens above
but within us
and within those
about us.

If we walk on this path
with faith,
we will feel God's presence
here in this room,
here in our hearts,
giving us strength,
guidance and hope.

"When you call Me, and come and pray to Me
I will give heed to you. You will search for
Me and find Me, if only you will seek Me
wholeheartedly." *(Jeremiah)*

בָּרוּךְ אַתָּה, יְיָ, שׁוֹמֵעַ תְּפִלָּה.

We praise You, O God, who hears prayer.

HEALING

(Suggested by *Psalm 86*)

Give ear, O Eternal, to my prayer,
    heed my plea for mercy.

In my time of trouble I call You,
    for You will answer me.

When pain and fatigue are my companions,
Let there be room in my heart for strength.

When days and nights are filled with darkness,
Let the light of courage find its place.

Help me to endure the suffering and dissolve the fear,
Renew within me the calm spirit of trust and peace.

בָּרוּךְ אַתָּה, יְיָ, רוֹפֵא הַחוֹלִים.

We praise you, O God, Healer of the Sick.

EVENING PRAYER

הַשְׁכִּיבֵנוּ, יְיָ אֱלֹהֵינוּ, לְשָׁלוֹם, וְהַעֲמִידֵנוּ, מַלְכֵּנוּ, לְחַיִּים.
וּפְרוֹשׁ עָלֵינוּ סֻכַּת שְׁלוֹמֶךָ.
וְתַקְּנֵנוּ בְּעֵצָה טוֹבָה מִלְּפָנֶיךָ, וְהוֹשִׁיעֵנוּ לְמַעַן שְׁמֶךָ, וְהָגֵן בַּעֲדֵנוּ.
בָּרוּךְ אַתָּה, יְיָ, הַפּוֹרֵשׂ סֻכַּת שָׁלוֹם עָלֵינוּ, וְעַל־כָּל־עַמּוֹ יִשְׂרָאֵל וְעַל
יְרוּשָׁלָיִם.

The Shelter of Your Peace

Cause us, our Creator, to lie down in peace,
and raise us up, O Sovereign God, to renewed
life and peace. Spread over us the shelter of
Your peace; guide us with Your good counsel;
and be our shield of mercy and of peace.

We praise You, O God, whose shelter of peace
is spread over us, over all Your people Israel,
and over Jerusalem.

NIGHT PRAYER

May it be Your will that I lie down in peace and rise up in peace. Let not my thoughts, my dreams, or my daydreams disturb me. Watch over my family and those I love.

O Guardian of Israel, who neither slumbers nor sleeps, I entrust my spirit to You. Thus as I go to sleep, I put myself into Your safekeeping.

Grant me a night of rest. Let the healing processes that You have placed in my body go about their work. May I awaken in the morning, refreshed and renewed to face a new tomorrow.

We praise You, Adonai Our God, Ruler of the Universe, who closes our eyes in renewing sleep.

MORNING PRAYER

מוֹדֶה אֲנִי לְפָנֶיךָ, מֶלֶךְ חַי וְקַיָּם שֶׁהֶחֱזַרְתָּ בִּי נִשְׁמָתִי בְּחֶמְלָה, רַבָּה אֱמוּנָתֶךָ.

I give thanks unto You, O God,
That in mercy, You have restored my soul within me.
Endless is Your compassion;
Great is Your faithfulness.

I thank You, God, for the rest You have given me
through the night and for the breath that renews
my body and spirit. May I renew my soul with
faith in You, Source of life's healing.

בָּרוּךְ אַתָּה, יְיָ אֱלֹהֵינוּ, מֶלֶךְ הָעוֹלָם, עֹשֶׂה מַעֲשֵׂה בְרֵאשִׁית.

We praise You, Adonai Our God, Ruler of the Universe,
who renews daily the work of creation.

MORNING PRAYER

בָּרוּךְ אַתָּה, יְיָ אֱלֹהֵינוּ, מֶלֶךְ הָעוֹלָם, אֲשֶׁר יָצַר אֶת־הָאָדָם בְּחָכְמָה,
וּבָרָא בוֹ נְקָבִים, נְקָבִים, חֲלוּלִים חֲלוּלִים.
גָּלוּי וְיָדוּעַ לִפְנֵי כִסֵּא כְבוֹדֶךָ, שֶׁאִם יִפָּתֵחַ אֶחָד מֵהֶם, אוֹ יִסָּתֵם אֶחָד
מֵהֶם, אִי אֶפְשָׁר לְהִתְקַיֵּם וְלַעֲמוֹד לְפָנֶיךָ.
בָּרוּךְ אַתָּה, יְיָ, רוֹפֵא כָל־בָּשָׂר וּמַפְלִיא לַעֲשׂוֹת.

Blessed is our Eternal God, Creator of the
universe, who has made our bodies with wisdom,
combining veins, arteries, and vital organs
into a finely balanced network.

Wondrous Fashioner and Sustainer of life,
Source of our health and our strength, we
give You thanks and praise.

MORNING PRAYER

שְׁמַע יִשְׂרָאֵל: יְיָ אֱלֹהֵינוּ, יְיָ אֶחָד!

Hear, O Israel: The Eternal is our God,
the Eternal alone!

בָּרוּךְ שֵׁם כְּבוֹד מַלְכוּתוֹ לְעוֹלָם וָעֶד!

Blessed is the glory of God's dominion
for ever and ever.

MORNING PRAYER

וְאָהַבְתָּ אֵת יְיָ אֱלֹהֶיךָ בְּכָל־לְבָבְךָ וּבְכָל־נַפְשְׁךָ וּבְכָל־מְאֹדֶךָ. וְהָיוּ
הַדְּבָרִים הָאֵלֶּה, אֲשֶׁר אָנֹכִי מְצַוְּךָ הַיּוֹם, עַל־לְבָבֶךָ. וְשִׁנַּנְתָּם לְבָנֶיךָ,
וְדִבַּרְתָּ בָּם בְּשִׁבְתְּךָ בְּבֵיתֶךָ, וּבְלֶכְתְּךָ בַדֶּרֶךְ, וּבְשָׁכְבְּךָ וּבְקוּמֶךָ. וּקְשַׁרְתָּם
לְאוֹת עַל־יָדֶךָ, וְהָיוּ לְטֹטָפֹת בֵּין עֵינֶיךָ, וּכְתַבְתָּם עַל־מְזֻזוֹת בֵּיתֶךָ,
וּבִשְׁעָרֶיךָ.

לְמַעַן תִּזְכְּרוּ וַעֲשִׂיתֶם אֶת־כָּל־מִצְוֹתָי, וִהְיִיתֶם קְדֹשִׁים לֵאלֹהֵיכֶם. אֲנִי
יְיָ אֱלֹהֵיכֶם, אֲשֶׁר הוֹצֵאתִי אֶתְכֶם מֵאֶרֶץ מִצְרַיִם לִהְיוֹת לָכֶם לֵאלֹהִים.
אֲנִי יְיָ אֱלֹהֵיכֶם.

You shall love the Eternal your God with all your mind, with
all your strength, with all your being. Set these words,
which I command you this day, upon your heart.

Teach them faithfully to your children; speak of them in your
home and on your way, when you lie down and when you
rise up. Bind them as a sign upon your hand; let them be
a symbol before your eyes. Inscribe them on the doorposts
of your house, and on your gates.

Be mindful of all My Mitzvot, and do them: so shall you
consecrate yourselves to your God.

I, the Eternal, am your God who led you out of Egypt to be
your God; I, the Eternal, am your God.

MORNING PRAYER

אֱלֹהַי, נְשָׁמָה שֶׁנָּתַתָּ בִּי טְהוֹרָה הִיא! אַתָּה בְרָאתָהּ, אַתָּה יְצַרְתָּהּ, אַתָּה נְפַחְתָּהּ בִּי, וְאַתָּה מְשַׁמְּרָהּ בְּקִרְבִּי. כָּל־זְמַן שֶׁהַנְּשָׁמָה בְקִרְבִּי, מוֹדֶה אֲנִי לְפָנֶיךָ, יְיָ אֱלֹהַי וֵאלֹהֵי אֲבוֹתַי, רִבּוֹן כָּל־הַמַּעֲשִׂים, אֲדוֹן כָּל־הַנְּשָׁמוֹת.

בָּרוּךְ אַתָּה, יְיָ, אֲשֶׁר בְּיָדוֹ נֶפֶשׁ כָּל־חָי, וְרוּחַ כָּל־בְּשַׂר־אִישׁ.

The soul that You have given me, O God, is a pure one! You have created and formed it, breathed it into me, and within me You sustain it. So long as I have breath, therefore, I will give thanks to You, O Eternal my God and God of all ages, Ruler over all creation, God of every human spirit.

Blessed is Adonai, in whose hands are the souls of all the living and the spirits of all flesh.

PSALM 23

מִזְמוֹר לְדָוִד. יְיָ רֹעִי, לֹא אֶחְסָר. בִּנְאוֹת דֶּשֶׁא יַרְבִּיצֵנִי, עַל־מֵי מְנֻחוֹת
יְנַהֲלֵנִי. נַפְשִׁי יְשׁוֹבֵב. יַנְחֵנִי בְמַעְגְּלֵי־צֶדֶק לְמַעַן שְׁמוֹ. גַּם כִּי־אֵלֵךְ
בְּגֵיא צַלְמָוֶת לֹא־אִירָא רָע, כִּי־אַתָּה עִמָּדִי; שִׁבְטְךָ וּמִשְׁעַנְתֶּךָ הֵמָּה
יְנַחֲמֻנִי. תַּעֲרֹךְ לְפָנַי שֻׁלְחָן נֶגֶד צֹרְרָי. דִּשַּׁנְתָּ בַשֶּׁמֶן רֹאשִׁי, כּוֹסִי רְוָיָה.
אַךְ טוֹב וָחֶסֶד יִרְדְּפוּנִי כָּל־יְמֵי חַיָּי, וְשַׁבְתִּי בְּבֵית־יְיָ לְאֹרֶךְ יָמִים.

God is my shepherd, I shall not want.
God makes me lie down in green pastures,
Leads me beside still waters, and restores my soul.
You lead me in right paths for the sake of
Your Name.

Even when I walk in the valley of the shadow of death
I shall fear no evil, for You are with me;
Your rod and Your staff—they comfort me.
You have set a table before me in the presence of my
enemies;

You have anointed my head with oil, my cup overflows.
Surely goodness and mercy shall follow me all the
days of my life,
And I shall dwell in the house of God forever.

תפלה

אֲדֹנָי, שְׂפָתַי תִּפְתָּח, וּפִי יַגִּיד תְּהִלָּתֶךָ.

Eternal God, open my lips, that my mouth may declare Your glory.

בָּרוּךְ אַתָּה, יְיָ אֱלֹהֵינוּ, וֵאלֹהֵי אֲבוֹתֵינוּ, אֱלֹהֵי אַבְרָהָם, אֱלֹהֵי יִצְחָק, וֵאלֹהֵי יַעֲקֹב: הָאֵל הַגָּדוֹל, הַגִּבּוֹר וְהַנּוֹרָא, אֵל עֶלְיוֹן. גּוֹמֵל חֲסָדִים טוֹבִים, וְקוֹנֵה הַכֹּל, וְזוֹכֵר חַסְדֵי אָבוֹת, וּמֵבִיא גְאֻלָּה לִבְנֵי בְנֵיהֶם, לְמַעַן שְׁמוֹ, בְּאַהֲבָה.

GOD OF ALL GENERATIONS

We praise You, Eternal our God and God of all generations;
God of Abraham, God of Isaac, God of Jacob;
God of Sarah and Rebekah, God of Rachel and Leah;
great, mighty, and awesome God, God supreme.
Creator of all the living, Your ways are ways of love. You remember the faithfulness of our ancestors, and in love bring redemption to their children's children, for the sake of Your name.

— 14 —

AS ONE APPROACHES SURGERY (OR CRISIS)

God, You are with me in my moments of strength
and of weakness. You know the trembling of my
heart as the turning point draws near.

Grant wisdom and skill to the mind and hands of
those who will operate on me, and those who
assist them. Grant that I may return to fullness
of life and wholeness of strength, not for my
sake alone but for those about me. Enable me to
complete my days on earth with dignity and purpose.
May I awaken to know the breadth of Your healing
power now and evermore.

בְּיָדוֹ אַפְקִיד רוּחִי בְּעֵת אִישַׁן וְאָעִירָה,
וְעִם־רוּחִי גְוִיָתִי: יְיָ לִי, וְלֹא אִירָא.

My spirit I commit to You, my body, too, and all I prize;
Both when I sleep and when I wake, You are with me;
I shall not fear.

FOLLOWING AN OPERATION

Loving God, Your healing power has saved me. You have sustained me in my weakness, supported me in my suffering, and set me on the road to recovery. By Your grace, I have found the strength to endure the hours of distress and pain. God, give me patience and peace of mind. Help me, after I have recovered, to express gratitude for all Your mercies by greater devotion to Your service.

בָּרוּךְ אַתָּה, יְיָ, רוֹפֵא הַחוֹלִים.

Ba-ruch a-ta, A-do-nai, ro-fei ha-cho-lim.

We praise You, O God, healer of the sick.

O God, who provides us with processes of healing, I am grateful for your tender care. Help me to regain my health completely. Strengthen my body during its recovery, and ease my burdens of anxiety and pain. May I be blessed with Your comforting presence now and let my soul ever show forth my gratitude for the divine gift of life. Amen.

IN MY LONELINESS

There are often times, O God, when I feel alone, and yet I know in my heart that I am never alone. You are always there waiting for me to speak to You of my desires, hopes and dreams.

Yet how seldom do I reach out to You to voice my gratitude for all that is beautiful in my life. . . all the gifts of my life. Love, family, friendship have come from You.

But the greatest gift of all is Your presence, which time and again has given me strength, faith and courage.

Now, in the midst of doubt and confusion, I need to know that You are beside me in the depth of my being. With You there, I know I am not alone—ever.

My Friend, my strength, my God.

A PRAYER UPON RECEIVING GOOD NEWS

O God, how relieved and grateful I am for the good news I have received! Naturally, I was apprehensive—hoping for the best, but often worrying and imagining the worst. Thank You for being with me and enabling me to bear the tension and anxiety that were mine.

With the question marks behind, may I now devote my thoughts and energy to becoming healthier and stronger each day. Amen.

AN APPEAL TO GOD FOR FORGIVENESS

Out of the depths I call You, Adonai.
O God, listen to my cry;
let Your ears be attentive
to my plea for mercy.
If You keep account of sins, O God
Who will survive?
Yours is the power to forgive
so that You may be held in awe.

I look to Adonai,
My soul looks and awaits God's divine word.
I am more eager for the Eternal than watchmen for the
morning, indeed, more than watchmen for the morning.

O Israel, wait for Adonai
for with the Eternal is steadfast love and great power
to redeem.
It is God who will redeem Israel from all their iniquities.

A PRAYER FOR STRENGTH

O God, our refuge and strength, and an ever-present help in times of trouble, how much I need Your strength and presence in my life right now. I feel weak, depressed, anxious, even frightened. I need help to face these hours and days.

So I claim Your promises that I can bear whatever comes, that Your strength will be sufficient, and that my despair will give way to your peace that passes all understanding. Amen.

A PRAYER UPON RECEIVING BAD NEWS

God, You know the disappointment, the discouragement, the anxiety, the loneliness, yes, even the anger I feel because my prognosis is not good. I can only pray that You will give me and my loved ones the strength to face whatever lies ahead.

Don't let us panic. Let us be open and honest with one another, and enable us to make the most and the best of the coming days. Amen.

PSALM 121

אֶשָּׂא עֵינַי אֶל־הֶהָרִים, מֵאַיִן יָבוֹא עֶזְרִי? עֶזְרִי מֵעִם יְיָ, עֹשֵׂה שָׁמַיִם
וָאָרֶץ. אַל־יִתֵּן לַמּוֹט רַגְלֶךָ, אַל־יָנוּם שֹׁמְרֶךָ. הִנֵּה לֹא־יָנוּם וְלֹא יִישָׁן
שׁוֹמֵר יִשְׂרָאֵל. יְיָ שֹׁמְרֶךָ, יְיָ צִלְּךָ עַל־יַד יְמִינֶךָ. יוֹמָם הַשֶּׁמֶשׁ לֹא־
יַכֶּכָּה, וְיָרֵחַ בַּלָּיְלָה. יְיָ יִשְׁמָרְךָ מִכָּל־רָע, יִשְׁמֹר אֶת־נַפְשֶׁךָ. יְיָ יִשְׁמָר־
צֵאתְךָ וּבוֹאֶךָ, מֵעַתָּה וְעַד־עוֹלָם.

I lift my eyes to the mountains;
What is the source of my help?
My help comes from Adonai,
Maker of heaven and earth.
God will not let your foot give way;
your Protector will not slumber.
See, the Protector of Israel
neither slumbers nor sleeps!
God is your Guardian,
God is your protection
at your right hand.
The sun will not strike you by day,
nor the moon by night.
God will guard you from all harm
God will guard your soul,
your going and coming,
now and forever.

KEEPING PERSPECTIVE

O God, how helpless I feel! I am so dependent on my physician, my nurses, and all those who work in the hospital. I need medication to alleviate my discomfort and pain, and to help me rest. I'm not as strong as I was; I'm not as free as I was; I don't feel as well as I did.

But help me, O God, not to lose perspective. Keep me aware of the strength I do possess, what I am able to do, and the blessings that still are mine. Amen.

THE LONG DAYS

My God and God of all generations, in my great need I pour out my heart to You. The long days and weeks of suffering are hard to endure. In my struggle, I reach out for the help that only You can give. Let me feel that You are near, and that Your care enfolds me. Rouse in me the strength to overcome my weakness, and brighten my spirit with the assurance of Your love. Make me grateful for the care and concern that are expended on my behalf. Help me to sustain the hopes of my dear ones, as they strive to strengthen and encourage me. May the healing power You have placed within me give me strength to recover, so that I may proclaim with all my being: I shall not die, but live and declare the works of God.

A PRAYER OFFERED BY ONE AT THE BEDSIDE

O God, who are aware of my thoughts and feelings even before I share them, You know my concern for my loved one who is hospitalized. You know my apprehension and anxiety. You know how much I want my loved one to get well and be back home.

As You will be with my loved one during these days, be with me, too. Just as I will not neglect my dear one, may I not neglect myself. May I remember to eat enough and sleep sufficiently so that my health will be maintained, so that I can manage our household, and so that I can continue to attend to the needs of the one at whose bedside I pray. Amen.

A PRAYER FOR COPING

O God, you know my feelings, You know that I want to feel better. I want to be better. I want to have my health restored.

But the hours of testing, the days of diagnosis, and the question marks concerning my future seem nearly more than I can take!

Grant me, O God, the strength to face each hour of this and every day. In fact, when it seems that I cannot face even this hour, fill me with sufficient strength to face the next five minutes. Amen.

A PRAYER FOR PATIENCE

God, I'm tired of this whole hospital experience! In fact, I'm fed up with it. I'm bored. The days and nights just drag by. The routine of sleeping and eating, temperature and blood pressure taking, is about to get me down. The noise in the hallway bothers me, too. Not much seems to be happening. I want to go home!

You don't have to tell me—I know what my problem is. I need to be more patient. I can't expect to get well overnight. Healing takes time. Strength doesn't return with the snap of my fingers.

So, make me aware that if I can endure a little more and a little longer, these experiences will be behind me. And when I look back on them, they won't seem so frustrating as they do right now. Amen.

FOR FAMILY AND FRIENDS

Dear God, be with my family and friends. Bring peace to their troubled spirits. Enable them to know that their love gives me strength. Help me to express my gratitude and appreciation to them for all they have done and are continuing to do. Let them feel free to bring me their own joys and sorrows that I may continue to participate in their lives even as they share mine.

May this also be a time of inner searching, that I may appreciate more fully the good and beautiful in life and labor to bring these to the lives of others. Grant me health and healing that I may carry out Your will in peace. Then will my life reflect Your presence, and my love, Your love.

בָּרוּךְ אַתָּה יְיָ, רוֹפֵא הַחוֹלִים.

Ba-ruch a-ta, A-do-nai, ro-fei ha-cho-lim.

We praise You, O God, healer of the sick.

FOR MY CARE GIVERS

I thank you, God, for the skill, care and concern of the many about me who have dedicated themselves to health and healing. It is they who have had to respond to my calls for help; they who will be with me throughout the difficult times ahead. Grant wisdom, patience and understanding to them. Bless the work of their hands and their hearts that their labors may not be in vain. As Your helpers, may they find the way to restore me and others to a life renewed. May I and they feel the comfort of Your presence.

For health of body and of spirit, I thank You, God. I was broken and now I am whole. I was weary, but now I am rested. I was anxious, but now I am reassured.

I thank You for those who helped me in my need, who heartened me in my fear, and who visited me in my loneliness. For the strength You gave me, O God, I give thanks to You.

WAIT FOR THE ETERNAL

Wait for the Eternal.
Be strong, and let your heart take courage;
yes, wait for God.

A PRAYER BEFORE GOING HOME FROM HOSPITAL

O God, how glad I am to be going home! I'm grateful for this hospital and all who have cared for me, but how good it will feel to be back in familiar surroundings again and to sleep in my own bed again.

Grant me the wisdom and willingness to follow my physician's instructions during the coming days. Enable me to do all within my power to take care of myself so that I will not have to return as a patient.

Since I now realize how important contacts from my family and friends have been during my hospitalization, may I be more sensitive to the needs of others who are ill and let them know of my love and concern. And since You did not forget me during my illness, may I not forget You when good health is mine again! Amen.

A PRAYER DURING RECUPERATION AT HOME

How true it is, O God, that there is no place like home! I didn't realize how much I missed being among family and friends!

But now that I have been out of the hospital for a while, I'm beginning to feel restless. At times I'm bored. I'm anxious to be free from the restrictions that prevent the resumption of my usual schedule and activities.

Help me accept the fact that healing does not occur overnight, and that just as my illness developed over a period of time the regaining of my strength will take longer than I desire. Thus, may I be gracious and cooperative during my recuperation at home so that I will not upset and unnecessarily burden those who are caring for me now. And may I express my gratitude for their love and concern both verbally and in my actions. Amen.

A PSALM OF THANKSGIVING

O give thanks to God, who is good;
For God's love is everlasting.

In distress I called upon the Eternal; God answered me by setting me free.

With Adonai at my side, I am not afraid: what can mere mortals do to me?

The Eternal is my strength and my shield; God has become my help.

I shall not die but live and tell the deeds of the Eternal.

This is the day God has made; let us rejoice and be glad in it.